Prophetic Nature

...*Poems from an Open Soul*

Paige J. Thompson

PublishAmerica
Baltimore

© 2009 by Paige J. Thompson.
All rights reserved. No part of this book may be reproduced, stored in a retrieval system or transmitted in any form or by any means without the prior written permission of the publishers, except by a reviewer who may quote brief passages in a review to be printed in a newspaper, magazine or journal.

First printing

PublishAmerica has allowed this work to remain exactly as the author intended, verbatim, without editorial input.

ISBN: 978-1-60749-975-6
PUBLISHED BY PUBLISHAMERICA, LLLP
www.publishamerica.com
Baltimore

Printed in the United States of America

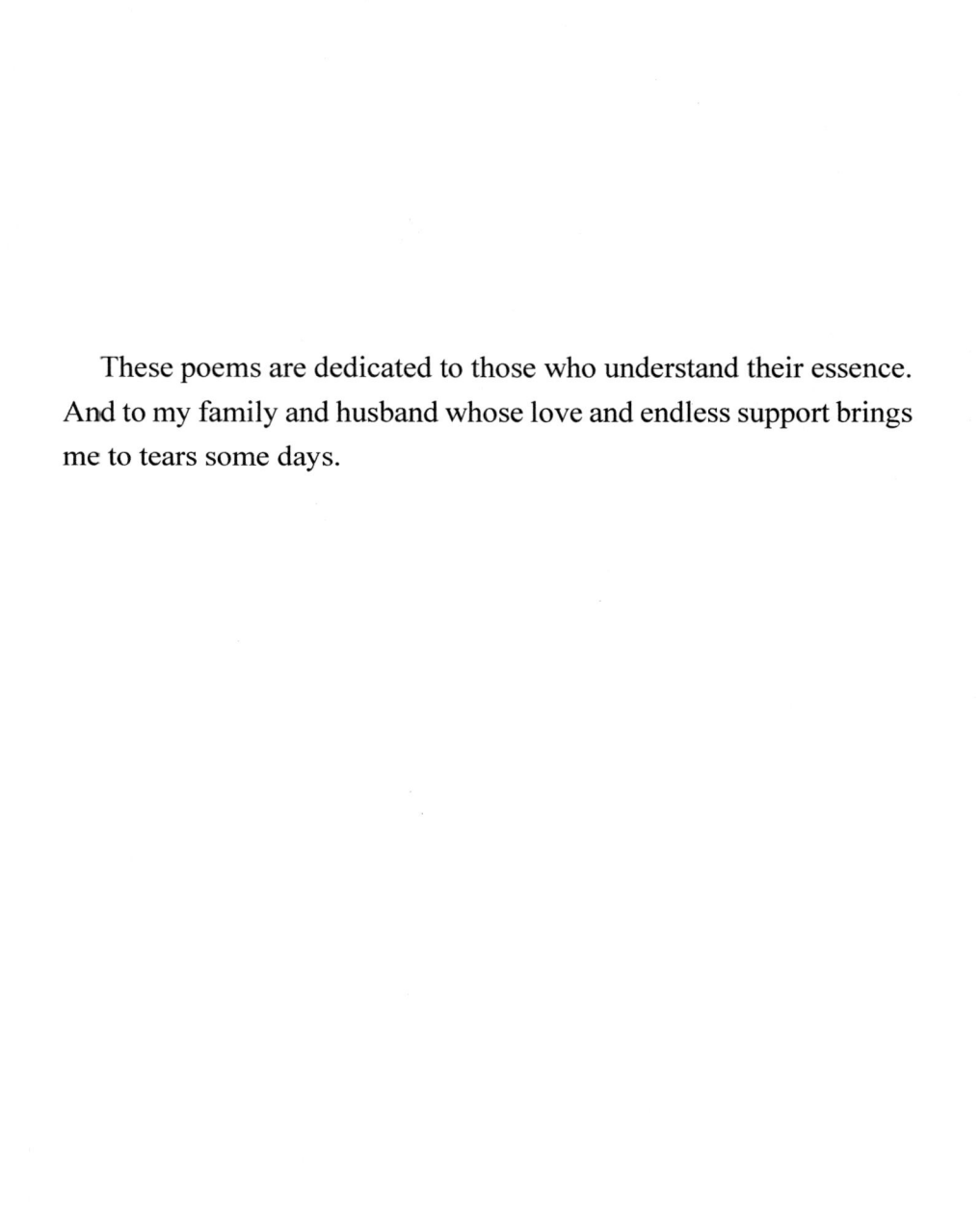

These poems are dedicated to those who understand their essence. And to my family and husband whose love and endless support brings me to tears some days.

I do not know where the words come from. They come from a place that I can only touch in dreams and meditation. They are fluid, subliminal, subconscious. They are messages and phrases that I am still learning to understand. Their meanings are concealed, dreamlike and interpretational, perhaps prophetic in nature. There are glimpses of past, present and future in their meaning. In discovering them I discover myself.

THOSE THAT WALK AMOUNG US

There are gods
that walk among us…

Secret and in shadows,
they vibrate to the "Om"
                  that they come from.
This is the echo that haunts them.
Makes strange in their delicate ears.
                  This is the sound that they scream to.
They sway this way and that to the sound
                  of their former selves.
They are mad with themselves.
Blinded by the rage of dethronement
their sounds plague them with half remembrance
                  and memory burns their souls.

Once they were.
Once they fell.
Once they will be again.

There are gods
        that walk among us,
           that many choose not to see.

                        Many like me.

MEANT TO BECOME

Who I am,
I still don't know.
I look into my eyes and see
          something I still don't understand.
I was told what I was suppose to be—
          Human. Humanness.
But why I do I feel like something more,
      like something less.
               Primal and free.
Part of tree, part of rain,
ground and sun,
animal and all.
    Not human.
    Not anymore.
I have evolved past myself.
I have evolved back to what we should have remained,
    and what we were meant to become.

WHAT EVE WANTED

I will bite the flesh,
        and tear the apple.
I will go back to my blood,
        and revel in original sin.
I will wrap warm scales around my shoulders
        and be proud of what I am,
        and where I have been.

This is what Eve had planned all along,
            since the beginning of the rib cage.

I HAVE NO NAME

I think of the forest
        and I am already there,

curled up in the sweet grasses and pollen of summer.
I am a wild thing once more.

Neither human, nor not quite animal.
I become a daughter unto myself.
I call the wolf and the deer by the same name.
I run with the wild things
and cry with the birds.

I think of the forest,
        and I am already there.

Rolling with the rain clouds,
and becoming untamed forever.

I hear the song of tribes long lost
and the buffalo running hard and fast.
I feel the spirit stir within me,
and at long last I am home.

Creature.
Animal.
Human.
What I am has no name.

LEFT

Where were you
        when I didn't know you?
Where were you
        when I didn't understand?
You brought me here,
You put me here,
Then left me here,
In a place, in a time,
        I don't understand.

It was simple then before you came.
It was simple still in my ignorance.

I wish I could go back.

WHAT IS MEANT TO BE

How far do I go
till I get to the end?
In the end
what will I be?

Just a composition
of paint and distraction.
Nothing but chocolate and horns.
I am more than skin and water.
But some days I like to be the dust.
Sometimes I'll play the prophet,
but more than not, the fool.
I will disagree with myself
and my self disagrees.
Am I the cosmic jester upon the stage?
I am the Coyote people
and the Buddha on his horse.

But some days I forget,
and skin suites me just fine.
Dragon fire no more,
today I will be the ashes.
Because I don't always want to go
where I have always been.
And how far do I have to go
before I cant come back?

I don't want to be what is meant to be,
I just want to be.

Be or becoming is a choice not made.
What am I?
    A little bit of everything
      held together with glue.

A HINT OF WHAT'S TO COME

Scribes will ask me
          in days to come,
'How do you know these things
          that you know?'
And I will answer with firm resolve…

I know.

STORM

There is a storm coming.
I can see it there.
I can see it there like an animal
      can smell its own death.
It is one that will
      shake the very core of my being.
A tragedy that makes heroes fall,
And men
      into myth.
It is a sour wind
      on my tongue.
I know it is coming
      because I have called it.

The presence that is I has made it arrive;
      since the dawn of my creation.
Now nothing can stop it.
Not even its Creator.

There is a storm coming.

ODD ALLY

Death,
walk with me
and hold my hand,
for I would rather have you as an ally
than an enemy.

THE RACE OF MEN

I am more than a bag of walking water.

I gave my blood to the earth,

And she gave her dust to me.

When did I become a herding animal

And join the race of Bag-o-Bones?

When did I loose the instinct,

Only to live in brick and idiocy?

I rejected the blood that was my gift.

I turned my back to the dirt.

I took up concrete and steal beams

To join the race of men.

THE GREAT LIGHT

Finally the Buddha inside me is awakening.
A germination,
        of a planted seed.
An orange seed that fell from a fig.
My light has turned
        from white to gold,
As fate hurls me through time,
        through space,
That is governed by moving orbs
That have a great light of their own.

MUD ANIMAL

I am a stationary
            ground animal.
My belly mired in the muck.
            Like a serpent I will crawl
Cause I was told salvation hides in humble dirt.

I have refused to see…
My polish has rubbed matte.
Sunlight is just an endless dream,
            a half memory,
                      something I was told about as a child.

I used to think I was special.
A part of a star—
            a grand design.
Now I realize I'm only human.
            with my ass in the mud.

THE CALL

I can hear their calling
>from deep inside my blood.

A roaring furry.
A hybrid wind.
Who are they that urge the primal call?
A brethren of forest things?
A pack of living memories?
What is the song
    that drives me to the edge of frenzy?
It is a consuming fire,
A beat that breaks upon my ears.
    This is all I see.
    This is all I know.
It is my call to feed the flame.
A call that has condemned me since the action of breath.

BOUND TO SOUND

I hear it,
it shakes the core of my being.
They give me names
to define my unfamiliar substance:
Malach.
Daemon.
Nephilim.
They forget I am bound to my sound.
Still a mortal amongst the apes,
the person who belongs to the Nowhere Tribe.
There are days when I and my shakes are one,
and there are days with only the shivers.
Oh Adoni, do you know what you have done?
Are you aware of my aware?
I have moved beyond mud into your house.

DREAMSPEAK

Anavrin.
Aipotu.
Esidarap.
reffo I tahw sI
ylno d'uoy fi uoy
.netsil

When a prophet speaks,
their words…
      their words go unnoticed
     and unheard.
Dreamwords are their language.
Truth—their magic!

TRUTH

Ambiance and a little bit of sacrifice
is all a soul needs to be complete.

THE LAND

The land is quiet.
The land is quiet.

She is hushed into stillness
       by a breath of silence.

And the wind sweeps across her face
       to close her mouth.

She forgives
but she does not forget.
And she is a poet at heart.

All is quiet now.
All is quiet.

I am home.

HOME

I can taste your earth.
I can taste your salt.
I have moss in my veins because of you.
If I were to fall right now,
> my skin would become pure wind.

Because of you I returned home.

This poem is for you.

TRUTH II

These are only words.
These are just words.
Injury is more likely
        with the pages they are written upon.

So why do you persist to flinch
        when dealing with them?

Truth hurts.

GAIA

I am but a visitor here.
My journey here is not long.
But where I go from here depends on you.

I am you.
I am your now.
I am the hopes and the dreams of your kind.

I see what you do when you think no one is looking.
                I am the one with many eyes.
And I hear what you say to each other when you think it is silent.
                I am the one with many ears.

There us a heart beat to this world.
And it is **I** who cry out to you.
I who cannot be seen
                cannot be heard.

Many eyes are blind.
Many ears are deaf.

            …and they are not mine.

YOU

You are the who, when I ask,
                'who is it?'
You are the where, when I ask,
                'well, where are you?'

How,
    is it that you came to be?

Why,
    is it you still follow me?

              Leave me alone.

PAINTED HANDS, PAINTED HORSE

The summer comes upon me.
   Painted hands, painted horse.
Delicious sun ripened skin
   of both the fruit and the flesh.
Bark splinted and wheat whipped,
   my nature is of this place.
My swan song calls me home.

Wind washed barely.
Sun sickened sweet grass.
A pollen yellow sun
    sets,
   and rises,
  against a bear sky touching a naked earth.

And rain will sweep it all and make it clean.

    I set my life to this song.

This song moves me.
This place haunts me.
The silence of it all stills me.
These fields have never been a forgiving place.
Even the asphalt is reclaimed by the grain.
Painted hands.
Painted horse.
I beg to hear the silence of this place.

ILLUSION

See past all that you are.
Smoke and mirrors of the truth.
All that is holy is here.
Bless your Name.

Am I as you dreamed me to be?
All is illusion.
I am not real.

I AM

Pensive.
Quiet.
Still.
In the cold.
In the dark.
In the silence of your breath,
You will know yourself.
You will know the Truth.
You will know a new name for God.

HUMAN BEING

Human. Being
what I'm supposed to be is
Human. Being
what I have always been is
Human. Being.
Human is being
Me.

DREAMS

A tortured soul dreams of clouds.
A king dreams of swords.
A girl dreams of what could be.
And a poet dreams of birds.

And what do I dream of?

I dream of swords
Cutting through the clouds
Like birds.

I am the girl who would be king.

MEMORY CRITIQUE

The past is on the tip of my tongue.
> Ready to break away and run.
>> I am a memory captured and bottled.

I have a secret self
> Which mirrors cannot reveal.
> Do you know me?

Do you want to know what I know?
> Reach in and grab my heart
>> And you will belong to me.

Truth lies in puddles that dry in the sun.
> I wait for answers to questions long ignored.
> The past keeps me from the future.

Daemon, they name is Memory.

THE HUNTING

Even though I am here,
I am out there
Amongst the trees
Chasing down deer.

I hunger for something I can't explain…
A food I've never tasted?
A drink I've never swallowed?
What is it that drives me to this,
This appetite for a thing I've never known?

Inside this room I am still a pack of wolves.
The people will watch me pace my cage
Of wallpaper and potpourri.
And I'm incomplete inside these walls that hide,
That confine and strangulate.

I am still out there.
And sometimes you can see me,
Dancing around the trees,
When the moon is round.
And the hunt is carried on with the sound of fleeting deer.

Even though I am here.
I will always be out there.

THE CHILD OF ALL

All is in this place.
Bless your name.

I am the child of All.
I am of all religions.
I am the first and last.
What is and what will be.
I am—
For I am of all people,
I am the soul of all.
I am the beginning and the end.
A child of the universe.

I am what I am because I am:
Sunchild.
Moonchild.
Dark and Light child.
I am the child of crucifixion.
I am the Nirvana child.
I am a child of glamour and incantation.
I am of all things—
For I am all.

From the dawn of time, till the end of time.
I will be.
Forever be.

AN HONEST TRUTH

"A house divided against itself cannot stand—"
                    and so the world will fall.

We have built ourselves on the sand.
The tide cometh.

*Line quoted from Abraham Lincoln

CHRISTA

She's got her hand on her mouth
                as she try's to hide a smile.

She's clutching her face
                like she wants to tear it off.

Does she want to show everyone
                what's underneath?

Is it a skull
        or something else?

PARALLEL ME

A little voice telling me,
        "I am great."
Another voice telling me
        "I am not."
What should I believe in?
Which mirror do I pick?
A parallel me?
A paradox…

I don't understand.
I am the blind man who can see.

THIS NIGHT

Tonight is the night
        where we talk of gods and men.
How men can act like gods,
        and how gods can be as men.
What is "deep?"…you ask.
        Is it a frame of mind?
Deep is me.
Deep is you.

And on this night,
        we ran as fast as we could.
Moving past ourselves,
        through ourselves.
Yet never from where we started.
Mine was a kind of real you couldn't see.
        …well, so was yours, but mine was heavier.

In that cold night,
        we became like gods.
And the gods came down to join us,
        in the guise of street lamps.
And each mailbox was a dream
        in which dangerous secrets where kept;
Each number a hidden passageway.
You said it was bending religion.
I said it was a higher awareness.

      You in the cube.
      I in the sphere.
You in your apocalyptic heaven.
I in my personal purgatory.

As you drove away,
        in your cow hide seated interior,
I wondered,
        what would happen to the corners of your cube
if only you knew what I knew?

That night we were like gods.
Yet we longed to be as men…

        …take no offence to these words my friend.

DEATH

Time has no meaning,
as night
stretches
on for eternity
making forever
only an instant.

RETURN TO YOU

I have tasted your exotic
        coffee's.
I have sat in your dark
        theatres.
And I have seen skyscrapers
        pull down an angry red sky.
And I want none of it!
I will not have it.
No none.

I will return to the places from when'st
        I came.
I will go to the woodlands and speak the tongue
        of birds for you.
And I will tell you of a place where the dead walk
        on paved roads.
And where they re-create the heavens
        with traffic lights.

And I will leave them all to return
        to you.
Just you.
  You with the grasses in your hair.

Yes, I will have none of it.
No none.

THE GREAT "OM"

We all cone from the Great "Om,"
The Hindu hum,
The strange echo,
The universal sigh.

Good or bad we vibrate to the same,
The sound that unifies us all.
No borders, no boundaries,
Just the sound where we came from…
                                    The Great "Om."

THE WOMAN OF NONE

Do not define me.
For what I am, you will never know.
I am not.
For I am nothing of your labels.
I am nothing of the weaker.
Because I am no part of you.

I was the Child of All,
Now the Woman of None.
For I am not part of you.
I am none.

I am the original—
Original sin made from apple seeds.
The first of many.
The last of All.

I am a new thing,
An old thing.
Something remembered,
And half forgotten.
I am not.
I am none.

A little bit of hell,
A little bit of earth,

Even less of heaven…
                An Axis Mundi.

WHERE THE WORDS ARE FOUND

The earth,

she screams,

as dark ground opens up to swallow cold steel.

And she chokes,

on black water bile
and her cries are stifled by drying cement.

This is where the poems come from.
This is where my words are found.

                        Not quite life and not quite death.

CALLED

Whirling,
Spiralling,
Dancing in a place unknown.
I was sent to you as the sword,
but I will appear to be as the rose.

Weaving,
Wanting,
The way of truth.
I will be a light against the dark,
a sheep among wolves.

A call has been sent forth.
My arrival has precedence.
This life will not be forgotten.
Things will be different.

THE FREED

Any wild thing caught,
caged,
will die.
The dove breathes for the sky.
The flame licks only the face of the freed.
The suffering servant knows not its need.

But if caged the voice is silent,
the soul turns violent.

CHILDREN OF MAN

In the dark
and in the silence
is where we will find each other.
When hope is gone,
when eyes weep dry,
we will know ourselves then.
There will be no more hindrance.
There will be no more hate.
We will feel each other there,
and feel only the same.
We will no longer be alone.
We will no longer be helpless.
We will stand in unity.
As a species.
As a humanity.

PROPHET

Fig and Lavender.
Milk and Honey.
That is what the holy ones smell off.

Time and incense.
Parchment and ink.
Is the smell carried on their breath.

Spice and smoke.
Fire and Dance.
Is what they move too.

Their nature is not a nature for us to understand.
Theirs is a song in a tune that we may never hear.
Honour them.
Love them,
Before they are claimed by the dust
And lost to time…

…forgotten…

SEEING THE COLOR

The life I breathe is the life I discover.
The essence of mortality drips off of me.
I am made a new.
My life made free.
Soul becomes guided by soul.
Spirit becomes free in spirit.
No more am I left to struggle
       with the emptiness of form.
Now I have learned to love the silence of one,
       the core of nothing, and the completeness of all.
I contain the flavour of being,
       the richness of life.
I am possessed by the universe in its entirety.
I have become the temple to which I pray.
Now I am seeing the colour
       of the universe that I have been placed in.
I have passed beyond the gates of uncertainty,
       and have carved out my own truth.

I am here…

       and I am STILL alive!

ANCIENT

Why is it when I try to forget,
I can remember the taste of the desert?
When I close my eyes
I can hear the sound of splitting wood?

HOW IT WAS

I remember you,
before the world changed your name.

I knew you,
before you became Latin.

I sought you out,
before you became paper,
an idea.

The world claimed you,
and I was forgotten.

You became parchment,
and I became dreams.

Your name was claimed,
mine became a whisper.

Unclean.
Dishonourable.
Profane.
Me.

Glorious.
Consecrated.

Sanctified.
You.

We were once on the same page.

SYMBIOTIC

Unearth…
      exposed.

The Earth…
      my backbone.

AEON

House of the Free Spirit.
Walker between the Worlds.
The 'All That is Here is Holy'.

Existence.
Sired by Time.
Mothered from Being.
A healthy mix of concept and technique.
Wisdom.
Breath.
Life.
The life that is the life of All.
The universe is on her back.

From the womb of subsistence she was called forth.
From the cradle of life she was nursed by the sound of creation.

Now…
    She can smell her own humanity.
    Her scent was stolen.
    The journey has brought her here.
    The path she walks mired in mortality.
    Swallowed down, watered down divinity.
    A shadow of truth…
    A reflection of absolute…

Love them when they have no love to give.
You bleed for the world.
Sophia—

                        Word made flesh.

IGNIS FATUS

You where veracious in your pursuit of the knowledge
    of my moral make-up.
You were simply something being simply something.
You weren't singing,
You were simply going through the motions of speaking fluidly.
Is this existence to you?
Is this what it is to be alive.
To copy the existence of something else?
You aren't you.
You were never you.
You were always feinting me.

ALTRUIST

Saint;
heart in chest, exposed.

Streetwalker;
    saint at heart, undisclosed.

The world will never know about you,
    messiah to the few.

LIGHTED

…the light spilling out like water…

        Sometimes I dream of bleeding.
    All I have belongs to the world.
    I pool all my fluids at my feet.
All I am belongs to everyone else.

I am a Buddha in waiting.
  I ride the liquid light.

      Even when I am standing still I am still dreaming

MY PRAIRIE PLACE

Like a poet at a loss for words,
I have been caught in a moment that requires none.

You have brought me to a place of no speech.

I was brought to this land in the arms of a great wind.
My sun,
My moon,
Set as one.
My time is no time here.
My place is a listening place of wild grasses.
Here I am absolved.
Here I am invented.

She is home,
        And the land doth sing…

INTIMACY

The bodies,
that bump and scrape in the night,
playing out poems of insight
on thighs of lovers in lamplight.
The songs of fever rush out in flight.

And lost,
are those in the gloom.
The flesh they exhume
as they clutch in the bedrooms,
—How they carve out their tombs.

They know not,
what is love…
for when push comes to shove
they look to the bleak above
to search out a new dove.

And find,
they are empty inside
as though life had been a lie.
their truth was denied.
existence only implied…

But the truth,
is that life

    is only a mystery.
That love
    is only a history,
Solace cant be found,
on the thighs of the unsound
or the wails of the unnamed
who will bathe in your shame.

It is known,
only from soul.
No one makes you whole.
You must loose all control.
And when you finally consol
the pain that is you,
the pain that is me
you finally begin…

Love.

*Written with David Bowie's "Sweet Thing" playing.

BLACK FOOT BUDDHA

Black Foot Buddha,
Composer for a silent age.
Your vaginal passing was of music and sound.
An after thought of birth.
Black is starving in the night.
Foot instilled in perpetual passion.
Buddha spoke without a sound.
You are the spiders silk.

You came into this world one crawl space at a time,
Clutching at straws and angel wings.
    Your first breath was filled with fire,
Your first sight consumed by blue.
You were born with an apple seed in your mouth and a missing rib.

It's a little bit harder now.

URBAN MUSE

The wind comes to collect the old and wake the babies.
I go to bed with someone else's influence on my skin,
A stranger on a strange land.
Sometimes in the middle of the night I am sure I stop breathing.

There is a piece of myself that I can't throw away because it still
        smells like the wind and the trees.
Because of this I have become the Hyphenate.
Not one thing, but certainly something.
I have begun to undefine myself as something solid.
So I will sit in my six second of silence and wait…

        …and wait…

            …and wait…

17th OUZO POWWOW

It's you and me and the men you loved
        with an eavesdropping woman beside us.
Hey baby, crank it up!
        Driving the past away.
Scream singing and throat grabbing.
        Lets talk this through.
Lets go to the place around the corner
        it's for people with your kinda shoes.
We laughed so hard it drowned out the drumbeats,
        you had the smell of Ouzo on your breath.
"I am going to write a poem about this," I said.
The world needs to know necessary moments like this.
And I have.
And it does.

It was a powwow of two.
Just me and you
        and the men that you loved
                and an eavesdropping woman beside us.

SMALL TOWN HOLLYWOOD

The tattoos on her skin are like maps to the stars,
Each birthmark a constellation.
      She is Hollywood in a 600 populous.
           She is Hollywood in a family of 5.

Big screen and screaming,
Her body is like sheet music in the wind.
Eden was only a concept and God was just a word.
      Hollywood is only famous with the birds.

You were born with the stage already in your teeth.
But the fair-weather fans are a small town that won't buy the
                                          tickets.
      Hollywood has grown to big for her fish bowl.
           And she has such a forgettable face.

THE CREATIVES

Its not poetry
It's breathing out God.
Its not painting
It's Genesis.
It is because of this that you can make yourself a new deity every day
This is why society keeps us around.
People always want to see what God is up to next.

WARHOL-Y

God must have been an artist of biblical proportions.
His Warholian Holy Ghost is alone in the Factory.
Aquatinted people made from a godless machine,
Marketed and mass produced in furious colours.
This is His fifteen minutes of fame.
I will hang Him on my wall.
We try to sell Him for millions and pass Him off as author.
Did He really do anything?
Maybe it's the people that named Him creator.
Perhaps creations created creator.

THE GREAT MASS PRETENDER

Today,
I have decided
I am going out in the ether.

No more cars.

No more coffee shops.

I can make it all disappear.

Do you know what reality is?
Do you know what truth you are in?

Now is the time.
This is the place.
        Move.

You have arrived.

You've always fit best as a mere idea more than you fit into
                                           your own life.

BEAST

The city,

      It fucking ruins everything.

            It lacks memory.

Does it even remember its name?
Or the spot in once had in paradise?

Like a beast on its back
It submits to our presence.
And like a beast it pisses on everything it disdains.
You cut off its head and the body still pumps life into the carcass.

Why do we stay here?
Why do we collect here
In masses like scabs and sores
On the backside of this concrete monster?

Surely we know better.
Surely we can amputate ourselves.
And yet,

      And yet…

We stay.

Humanity has always united together under a common enemy
                                          better
                                                              than it has its own positive nature.

THE VISITOR

You can't catch a lie from the one with Truth on her wrist.
Embracing the strange,
creating the life.
You have seen her before, but you can't understand her.

My confessional:

"Every breath
of every moment of existence,
I am here.
I see what an outsider sees.
I observe what a visitor observes.
My truth,
my nature,
is beyond yours.
Not above,
only further out.
I see the energy of being,
where sometimes only emptiness can be found.
I am the visitor to you,
and I am not like you.
Not above,
just further out.
Out and away."

It was in that moment that you found the face of your ancestors.

Also available from PublishAmerica

EDUCATING ANDREW
By Virginia Lanier Biasotto

The strongest bond in the animal kingdom is mother and offspring.

When something threatens, the mother instinctively acts to protect. The story of Andrew is a human example, and the enemy was one of our most revered institutions: the public school.

For most children, the beginning of school is a time of anticipation and excitement. New clothes and supplies are purchased. A preliminary visit to the classroom sets the stage for the promise, "This is where you will learn to read." For Andrew, the reading part didn't happen. For seven years solutions were sought, found and rejected. The printed page remained a mystery. The effects of his failure to read were dire. Andrew's love of life had been taken away, and his parents and teachers were helpless to do anything about it.

Paperback, 132 pages
5.5" x 8.5"
ISBN 1-4241-0171-9

When it appeared that Andrew would remain illiterate as he entered junior high school, a door opened that would change his life and that of his mother forever.

About the author:

VIRGINIA (GINGER) LANIER BIASOTTO is a native of Delaware and a graduate of the University of Delaware (1959). She is the founder of Reading ASSIST® Institute and the author of ten Reading ASSIST® text books. In 2005, Virginia received Delaware's Jefferson Award for Public Service for her contribution to literacy. She and her husband, Lawrence, are semi-retired and spend half of each year in Wilmington, Delaware, close to children, grandchildren and mothers, and the other half in Palm City, Florida.

Available to all bookstores nationwide.
www.publishamerica.com

Also available from PublishAmerica

RETURN TO THE ASHAU
By John James Kielty

A most secret plan by the U.S. Government to prepare for a pullout from Vietnam was initiated in 1968 just after the momentous Tet Offensive. The plan called for the caching of great treasure to support the expected network of spies that would stay behind. The Green Beret soldiers who unknowingly planted these treasure troves learned of its existence and now they were determined to retrieve it. The officials who directed these missions in the past were now holding higher offices and were ambitiously seeking even higher positions. The American public could not be allowed to find out about the government's plan to cut and run and the needless deaths of thousands of our young men and women who fought and died for a cause already determined to be without merit. When these government officials learn of the covert plans of these men to retrieve this treasure, they decide this cannot occur and the deadly decisions are made. The chase begins and with it the treachery and lies.

Paperback, 358 pages
6" x 9"
ISBN 1-4241-2124-8

About the author:

John James Kielty spent twenty years as a warrior soldier, or as the Irish would call him, one of the Wild Geese. Though born in Ireland, he fought in America's wars proudly and with distinction. John James Kielty is proud of the great heritage of Irish writers with whom he shares a love of the written word. He now lives in semi-retirement in the rural mountains of southern West Virginia that are so much like his native Ireland in appearance. He spends his free time working with wood and periodically sitting at his keyboard.

Available to all bookstores nationwide.
www.publishamerica.com

Also available from PublishAmerica

THE SEED OF OMEGA
By Eugene Ettlinger

The Seed of Omega depicts the molding of rural Palestine from the windblown nomadic land of weeds and sand into a Mecca in the Middle East. The land was populated by assimilation through different cultures, which includes an ethnic invasion after the soil had been tilled. A greater understanding of political power through favored in-migration status shows the melding of a select society. The power brokers governing the land became subservient to the will of neighboring nations in exchange for the production of oil. The cast is composed of variations of the Middle Eastern Arab people, the power brokers of the British Empire and the exiles from hostile nations the world over.

Paperback, 511 pages
6" x 9"
ISBN 1-4137-8882-3

The diversity of characters represents different walks of life to be filled by the shoes of the reader. They fought for survival and a love for one another. They were dedicated to the building of a society while struggling to implement a diverse nation running from a past life simply to find a place in which to be. Their fears are offset by the courage to survive in the creation of a nation.

About the author:

A native New Yorker and Fordham University graduate, Gene Ettlinger performed graduate studies in the field of sociology. Gene's dedication is in the development of community life. Growing up in the mixing bowl of ethnic diversity led to his keen interest in the alienation of unskilled workers. Gene is a pilot, skier, skilled boating enthusiast, and an accomplished artist. He currently resides in New York and Florida.

Available to all bookstores nationwide.
www.publishamerica.com

Also available from PublishAmerica

SIOBHAN
An AI's Adventure

By Emma L. Haynes

Siobhan: An AI's Adventure is a story that follows an android from his creation to his death. His most important mission is to pilot a colony ship filled with one hundred humans to a new planet, where he is to become a simple computer. A colonist tries to kill Siobhan before they land at their destination. This disruption causes the colony ship to shoot past the desired planet and crash land on a planet of an advanced race. Siobhan and only three humans survive. Fighting off attacks from the locals, Siobhan gets them off the planet.

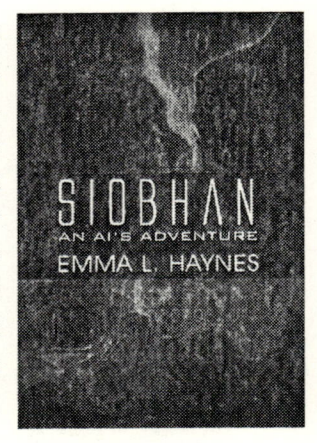

Paperback, 176 pages
5.5" x 8.5"
ISBN 978-1-60749-130-9

About the author:

Emma L. Haynes lives in North Pole, Alaska. She is married to an Army soldier and has one son. Through the years, she has enjoyed writing poetry, science fiction, fantasy, and historical fiction. She plans to travel the world when she gets the chance. She has one book published entitled *Poems from the Heart*. Visit her website at www.EmmaLHaynes.com.

Available to all bookstores nationwide.
www.publishamerica.com